AMERICAN INGENUE

Conway

GW00360681

ISBN: 978-1-913642-36-5

The author has asserted their right to be identified as the author of this Work in accordance with the Copyright, Designs and Patents Act 1988

Book designed by Aaron Kent

Edited by Aaron Kent

Broken Sleep Books (2021), Talgarreg, Wales

CONTENTS

"If she's Jessica, then who am I?"
Sweet Valley High #7 *Dear Sister*

"Look how black the sky is,
the writer said.
I made it that way."
Bret Easton Ellis, *Lunar Park*

American Ingénue

Cathleen Allyn Conway

PROLOGUE: DISAPPEAR HERE

Today I strangled my twin sister—
not a pleasant way to wake up.

She is the distraction I needed:
her chalky face, her purple-lined

mouth; her chopstick legs and bony
knees and a head like someone stuck

a pumpkin on a neck.
I loved her in dreams,

blah-coloured eyes and hair
a dull yellow mess of split ends.

Her throat tightened,
my throat tightened,

and I faced the skyline. Reached
again into my bag of sorrows.

This is how life presents itself in New York,
maybe anywhere, at the end of the century:

LIZ THAN ZERO (1)
I'M SITTING IN CASEY'S

in a booth near the window, waiting, white as a sheet.
It doesn't take long to get brown in this weather.

I ask the waitress for a mug of root beer, but she
doesn't bring me anything, just wipes the next table.

A small, sweaty guy in a Universal Studios t-shirt sits
two booths away. He's staring, hot from the airport drive.

He keeps staring. There is only one logical way out
of this mess: zipping around New York in his Ferrari!

Moonlight sails on his father's yacht! Debutante
balls! Skiing! Saying hi to King Kong! I look down.

He says he bets my boyfriend has trouble keeping up
with me, like trying to choose a flavour of ice cream.

SHOPPING

The people I have to buy presents for are
my twin Lizzie, two friends, my mom, my dad,
and my brother Steven. Right now I am moving down
Madison Avenue after spending an hour standing
in a daze near the staircase at Ralph Lauren on 72nd,
staring at cashmere sweater vests, confused, hungry;
when I finally take hold of my bearings, I'm not whirling
breathlessly in the flashing lights of Tunnel, Mick Jagger
isn't touching my arm and saying, *Pardon me, this next
dance is mine;* an agent is not proclaiming me the Next
Top Model, nor will my face be on the cover of *Ingenue*
within weeks. Strolling Tiffany's glittering aisles, no one
rushes up to say, *look how the jewels match your blue-green
eyes! It is a gift to see you wear them.* I leave, yelling *I am
ready for New York, but is New York ready for me?!* and
move down Fifth to Saks, emeralds tingling my spine.

LIZ THAN ZERO (2)
I DRIVE TO TODD'S HOUSE,
BUT HE ISN'T THERE

and so I sit in his room
and put a movie in the Betamax

and call Steven
and ask him if nuts are sensitive to cracks

and does it matter
and he says, 'turn sideways and stick out your tongue; you could
pass for a zipper'

and I draw on a piece of paper that's next to the phone
and he says 'aren't you lucky to have a nice daddy'

and it was obviously a dismissal
and he says, 'I'm going to have trouble squeezing my head out the
door'

and I say 'I know'
and there's a long silence heavy with irony before he says 'okay'

and I say 'our blankets are besieged by boys'
and hang up.

DATE WITH EVELYN

I imagine the whole scenario quite clearly:
They are all drinking her parents' blueberry
cassis and Cristal when I arrive,
and Evelyn, a tall, sleek brunette in Anne Klein
and antique gold earrings that cost, roughly, 137
thousand dollars, gives a tinkly little laugh. 'Oh,
you mean like in *chaperone*?', and hands a glass
of plum wine to me. I can hardly stand up; the
room seems impossible, appears so much older.

If only I could have parties like this, with Evelyn
on Mars and her deafening whine a Maserati, her
father's cellar a big dizzy estate in Connecticut,
and sprawled in the backseat of an unappealing cab
I idly wonder if I should cut them up: fill the bath
with Evelyn, bump into tables of Malcolm, trip
over James, drink David like liquor from a glass.

LIZ THAN ZERO (3)
I'M WITH TODD

at the Dairi Burger in a yellow booth
made of lemons from the back yard.

We're waiting for Buzz, who is 15 minutes
late and never has boring vacations.

Todd's drinking a Pepsi. His Adam's apple
bobs in his scrawny throat and his ears

turn fire-engine red. Sometimes I think
he's too in love with me. It scares me.

He just shrugs. I don't like being a thin
layer of catsup spread on a burger bun.

I'm not hungry. Todd is impatient:
Pass me the mustard. Pass me the salt.

He waggles a pickle spear under his nose, says:
I don't see what's so crazy about falling for a foxy lady.

I stare out the window. The headlights
of passing cars are a threat. A promise.

SIGHTSEEING

I want to see him bleed.

I want to see blood bubble out his nose

I want to see him tied up with wire; his mouth, his face, his balls, all duct-taped

I want him to scream when I push

I want him to hear that I hate him, that he's the most awful person I've ever met

I want him to know New York doesn't compare to a new pair of culottes

I want to see him look like Prince Charming

I want him to hand me a glass, to kiss me

I want to see he has more in mind than kissing

I want him to slap my arms to the couch

I want his mouth on my throat

I want to see the lights blaze at my hostess's apartment

I want her to see I am gloved in her daughter's dress

but it is dark and chilly and the ride through Central Park isn't fun anymore.

LIZ THAN ZERO (4)
IT'S TWO IN THE MORNING

and hot
and we're at the Beach Disco

and Todd is trying on my sunglasses
and I tell him that I am a fair lady lost in a sea of iced tea

and I tense up every time the music stops
and the DJ passes out sizzling hamburgers of dry wit

and that the guy in the red leather pants over by the bar is so hot
and he must think I'm the klutziest girl in the whole world

and he stares like there's a movie star on his back lawn
and Steven gets all huffy

and says *Look* with a trace of annoyance but instead I look at Todd
and tell him again, *I am an old hag, a real witch*

and Todd says, *You're too much*
and I keep staring at my shoes, a fair lady lost in a sea of iced tea

TAXI DRIVER

This is all her fault:

Stuck in a gridlocked cab heading downtown,
the driver knocks on the plexiglass divider.

His smile is impenetrable. I put the Walkman
back on, but he motions to me.

My mouth tastes funny, like a croak throbbed up
from the pit of my stomach in drunk hiccups.

There's a long pause while he stares at me;
grim smile fading in the rearview mirror.

I see the locks lower in a flash,
hear the hollow clicking noise.

LIZ THAN ZERO (5) NOBODY'S HOME.

My room hasn't changed: the walls are still white, books in place,
Venetian blinds open as I left them, and on the wall, the poster

for O'Neill's *Touch of the Poet* starring Jason Robards, a wry, ironic
smile on his lips. Jason, why didn't you bring me something sexier?

Jason's eyes don't look at me. They only look at whoever's standing
by the window. The a/c is on and the house smells like pine.

Doctors in and out all day. Everything is totally wrong. Do you
believe how absolutely horrendous I look today, Jason?

I'm disgustingly fat, Jason, I swear: the skinniest legs in America,
bumpiest knees. You expect me to wear that, wash this stuff out

of my hair, take off all this makeup? I'm so gross, Jason.
Just look at me. I'm too tired to stand by the window.

THIS IS NOT AN EXIT

I'm getting sick. I am plastic.
There could be a telethon for
all the things wrong with me.
This is what we do to flee ourselves.
It's easier than being happy.

My mother cleaned out my closet.
This is what we do to please others.
She has her own sense of order;
you never know when her wicked gleam
will stare you into a tiny, shrinking smudge.

Everything was veiled while I was gone.
All night, stood here, a depressed pile
of notebooks floating two feet off
the pavement, another broken scene
in what passes for my life, my past
spelled out in toilet paper on the lawn.

EPILOGUE: AREN'T YOU HAVING A GOOD TIME HERE?

Why don't you tell me who I am,
if you know so much? Locate the

moment I became the damaged party girl
who wandered the wreckage of New York,

dead inside my perfect size-six life. It isn't
perfect, you know. My mother and brother

are out shopping. There's a note on the
Spanish-style kitchen table. It's so unfair

when people say mean things behind your back.
I can see the dog, Prince Albert, lying by the pool,

breathing heavily, asleep, his fur ruffled
by the wind. My mirror's faithless

reflection requires answers without questions,
inspires flickering thoughts of tired irony.

From my nose streams blood
of a vast, abandoned world.

NOTES AND ACKNOWLEDGEMENTS

These poems are found works from *Less Than Zero, American Psycho, Lunar Park* and *Imperial Bedrooms* by Bret Easton Ellis and the Sweet Valley High series by Francine Pascal, written by Kate William, specifically #11, *Too Good to Be True.*

The author is indebted to the editors of the following journals, where some of these poems first appeared: *Drunk Monkeys* and *Anthropocene Poetry.*

Additional thanks to those who provided feedback, advice and support during the drafting of this collection: Sarah Nichols, Kathryn Maris, Amy Bruinooge, and Jeanne Obbard, as well as Charlie and Aaron for their enthusiasm and support.

LAY OUT YOUR UNREST

Lightning Source UK Ltd.
Milton Keynes UK
UKHW020211160221
378827UK00006B/237